To Parents

This is a book for you to use **with** your child at the Sunday Eucharist—and you can start as soon as he won't automatically tear a book to pieces.

As early as possible encourage your child to join in, by saying Amen when he is tiny (even if he says it too late and very loudly—and this can be one of the first words he learns to say), by watching and by listening. Most of the text which he will have to say has been supplied in this book, because if you yourself speak and sing clearly a very young child can join in with the familiar words: explanations have been added in some places to help you focus the child's attention more directly towards ideas he can understand.

Do try to help him attend as much as possible by continually recalling him to what is happening: you will find in this way too that you can pay some attention to the service yourself, even though the child obviously occupies much of your mind.

This book is written in the hope that you will find it a help in your family worship.

Dear Jesus,

Thank you for letting us come to church to worship you. Help us to join with other people, to listen, to say the prayers and to sing the hymns —to your praise and glory.

Amen.

The Lord be with you.

And also with you.

We all join in

Almighty God,

to whom all hearts are open,

all desires known,

and from whom no secrets are hid:

cleanse the thoughts of our hearts

by the inspiration of your Holy Spirit,

that we may perfectly love you,

and worthily magnify your holy Name;

through Christ our Lord.   Amen.

Lord have mercy.

Lord have mercy.

Lord have mercy.

Christ have mercy.

Christ have mercy.

Christ have mercy.

Lord have mercy.

Lord have mercy.

Lord have mercy.

Glory to God in the highest
and peace to his people on earth.
Lord God, heavenly king,
almighty God and Father,
we worship you, we give you thanks,
we praise you for your glory.
Lord Jesus Christ, only Son of the Father,
Lord God, Lamb of God,
you take away the sin of the world:
have mercy on us;
you are seated at the right hand
    of the Father:
receive our prayer.
For you alone are the Holy One,
you alone are the Lord,
you alone are the Most High,
Jesus Christ, with the Holy Spirit,
in the glory of God the Father.   Amen.

Listen while the Collect is said: this is a
short prayer—a different one for
each Sunday or special day.
At the end we say

Amen.

We next listen to readings from the Bible.
First there will be a reading from the
Old Testament or the Epistle or both.
In each case at the end get ready
to say

Thanks be to God.

The person is reading to us from the Bible,
reading something which will tell us
about God—what he is like, what he
has done, what he wants us to do.

Glory to Christ our Saviour.

Praise to Christ our Lord.

We believe in one God,
the Father, the Almighty,
maker of heaven and earth,
of all that is seen and unseen.

We believe in one Lord, Jesus Christ,
the only Son of God,
eternally begotten of the Father,
God from God, Light from Light,
true God from true God,
begotten, not made,
one in Being with the Father.
Through him all things were made.
For us men and for our salvation
he came down from heaven;
by the power of the Holy Spirit
he was born of the Virgin Mary,
    and became man.
For our sake he was crucified under
    Pontius Pilate;
he suffered, died and was buried.

On the third day he rose again
in fulfilment of the Scriptures;
he ascended into heaven
and is seated at the right hand of the
    Father.
He will come again in glory
to judge the living and the dead,
and his kingdom will have no end.

We believe in the Holy Spirit, the Lord,
    the giver of life,
who proceeds from the Father and the
    Son.
With the Father and the Son he is
    worshipped and glorified.
He has spoken through the Prophets.

We believe in one holy catholic and
    apostolic Church.
We acknowledge one baptism for the
    forgiveness of sins.
We look for the resurrection of the dead,
and the life of the world to come. Amen.

Lord in your mercy

Hear our prayer.

Accept these prayers

for the sake of your Son,

our Saviour Jesus Christ.   Amen.

Almighty God, our heavenly Father,
we have sinned against you and
against our fellow men,
in thought and word and deed,
in the evil we have done
and in the good we have not done,
through ignorance, through weakness,
through our own deliberate fault.
We are truly sorry and repent of all
our sins.
For the sake of your Son, Jesus Christ,
who died for us,
forgive us all that is past;
and grant that we may serve you in
newness of life
to the glory of your Name.   Amen.

We do not presume

to come to this your table, merciful Lord,

trusting in our own righteousness,

but in your manifold and great mercies.

We are not worthy

so much as to gather up the crumbs

   under your table.

But you are the same Lord

whose nature is always to have mercy.

Grant us therefore, gracious Lord,

so to eat the flesh of your dear Son

   Jesus Christ,

and to drink his blood,

that we may evermore dwell in him,

and he in us.   Amen.

The bread and wine (and perhaps water)
are taken to the holy table, for us,
ready for the priest's special prayer in
a little while.

And also the money we have given—which
the priest may lift up so that we can
see we have given it to God.

We may then say
Yours, Lord, is the greatness,
the power, the glory, the splendour,
and the majesty;
for everything in heaven and on earth
is yours.
All things come from you,
and of your own do we give you.

The priest begins, and we reply

The Lord is here.
His Spirit is with us.
Lift up your hearts.
We lift them to the Lord.
Let us give thanks to the Lord our God.
It is right to give him thanks and praise.

The priest thanks God for making us, and for sending Jesus into the world for us.

We must listen to the special words which are said, and then join with the angels, thanking God and saying

Holy, holy, holy Lord
God of power and might,
Heaven and earth are full of your glory.
Hosanna in the highest.

... he took bread ...
he broke it, gave it to his disciples,
and said, 'Take, eat; this is my body ...'

He took the cup ...
and gave it to them, saying,
'Drink this, all of you; for this is my
     blood ...
Do this ... in remembrance of me.'

Christ has died:
Christ is risen:
Christ will come again.

**Blessing and honour and glory and
     power
be yours for ever and ever.   Amen.**

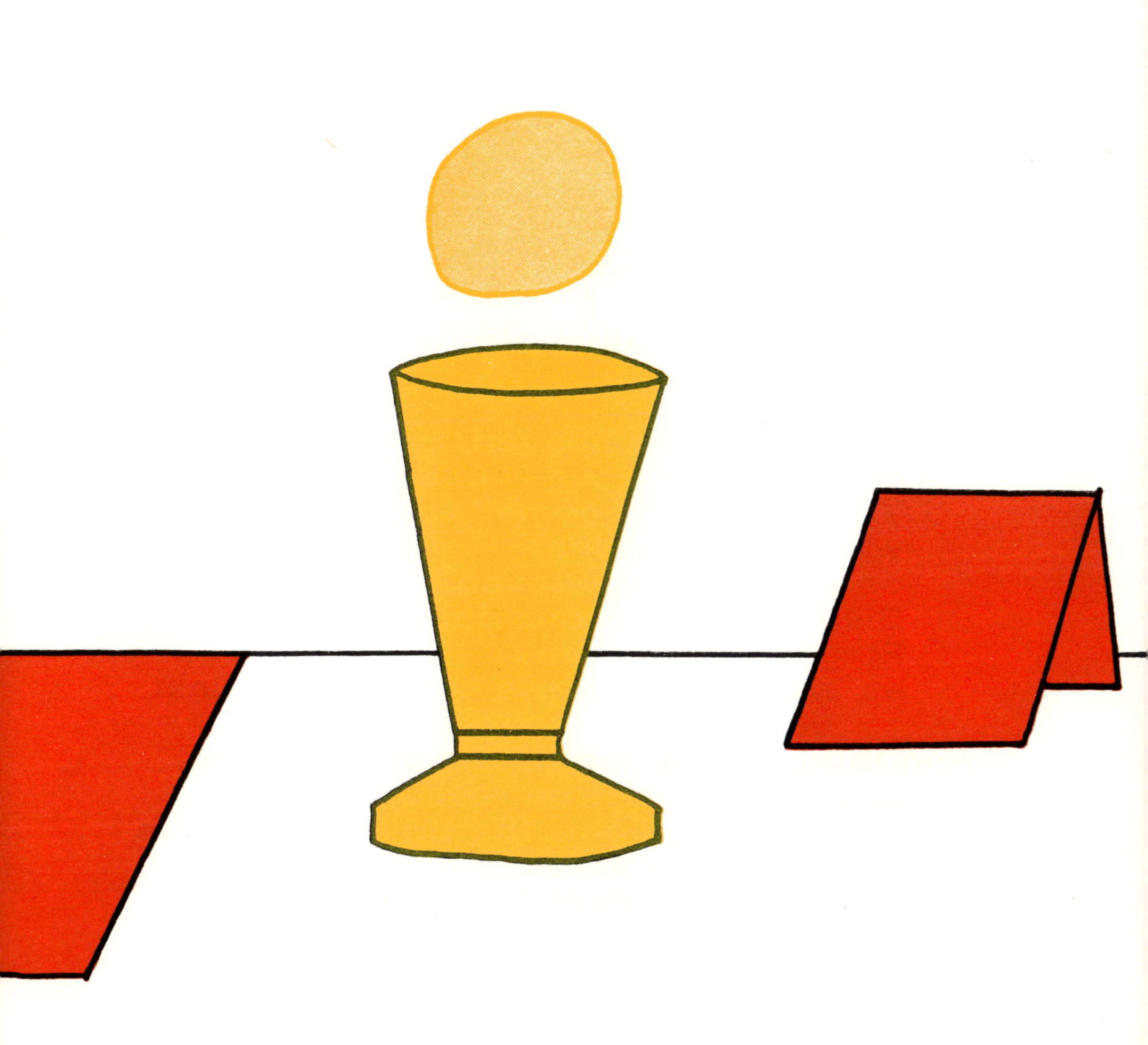

We break this bread
to share in the body of Christ.

Though we are many, we are one
body,
because we all share in one bread.

Our Father in heaven,
hallowed be your Name,
Your kingdom come,
your will be done,
on earth as in heaven.
Give us to-day our daily bread.
Forgive us our sins
as we forgive those who sin against
us.
Do not bring us to the time of trial
but deliver us from evil.
For the kingdom, the power, and the
glory are yours
now and for ever.   Amen.

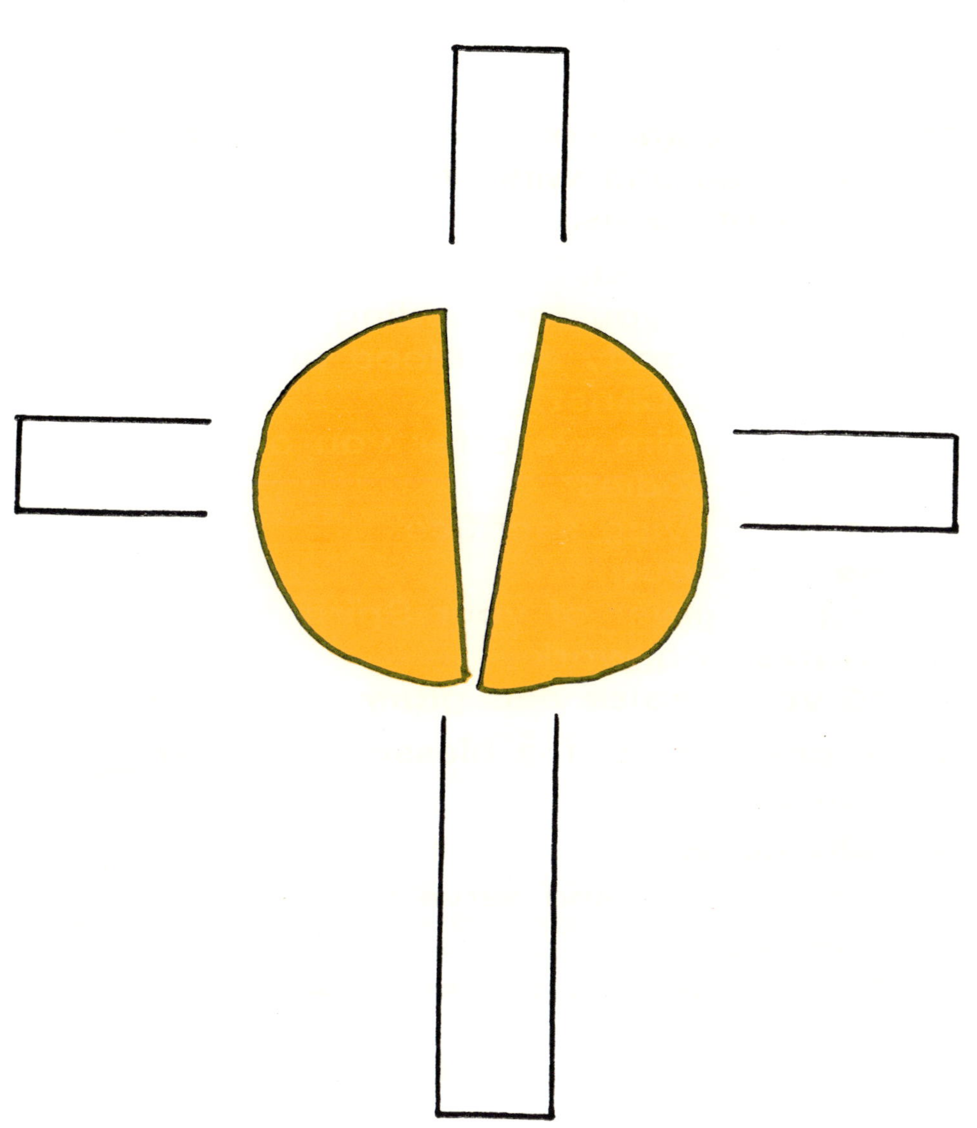

After the communion—we thank God for
the bread and wine, for the body and
blood of Jesus.

Almighty God,
we thank you for feeding us
with the body and blood of your Son
Jesus Christ.
Through him we offer you our souls
and bodies
to be a living sacrifice.
Send us out
in the power of your Spirit
to live and work
to your praise and glory.   Amen.

If the priest gives the blessing, we say
Amen.

He tells us to
Go in peace and serve the Lord
and we say
In the name of Christ.   Amen.